Scoring a Whole in One

People in Enterprise Playing in Concert

SCORING A WHOLE IN ONE

People in Enterprise Playing in Concert

EDWARD MARTIN BAKER

CRISP PUBLICATIONS

Editor-in-Chief: *William F. Christopher*

Managing Editor: *Kathleen Barcos*

Editor: *Shannon S. Pries*

Cover Design: *Kathleen Barcos*

Cover Production: *Russell Leong Design*

Book Design & Production: *London Road Design*

Printer: *Bawden Printing*

Library of Congress Card Catalog Number 98-74743

ISBN 1-56052-549-5

CONTENTS

ACKNOWLEDGEMENTS

I dedicate this book to Shige and Evan. They make my life whole.

I learned much from W. Edwards Deming, from his teaching and from his being. He revealed the wisdom that makes leadership possible.

The following people helped me to orchestrate this work. I thank them and recognize that they are not at fault if the book is not in concert:

Shige J. Baker, who knows how to play in the theater of business, and on the golf course as well

Evan Keith Baker for being Evan. He inspired and encouraged me in ways that he doesn't know

Anne Marie Borch, who knows how to make an artistic performance whole

Tom O'Connell, who knows how to make a golf performance whole, and helps others to do that

Terry Balderson, who is in the *Fifth Business* in the lives of his friends

Tom Johnson, who dares to "bring management to life"

Bill Christopher, who asked me to write the book, and helped me to keep the system in focus

Introduction

To understand the "Whole in One" idea of this book, it is helpful to keep in mind the definition of Whole: Whole: healthy; a coherent system or organization of parts fitting or working together as one.

Consider Golf

Every golfer has a model, a picture in mind that represents the proper swinging motion. Some models can produce excellent performance, others will produce poor performance. The model must be clear, complete and in harmonious relationship with the individual. The golfer should practice and play in an environment that is completely safe and free of intimidation.

Tom O'Connell
PGA Golf Professional
Scottsdale, Arizona

Serious golfers are always learning. They are able to experience that wonderful high, that magical feeling that comes when the swinging motion is a unified whole; everything is just right, in synch, together. There are no separate parts, no shoulders, arms, hands, hips, legs, or feet. They all interact as one to accomplish the purpose of the activity–to send the ball to the target, the hole. The hands don't try to dominate the feet. The arm swing doesn't dominate the body rotation. The eyes don't look wherever they please. Each part of the body that contributes to the purposeful action of swinging the golf club interacts harmoniously with the other parts, and with the golf club, in order to perform properly. It is as if the body as a whole *knows* what to do.

The interaction of the club with the ball and the consequent speed and direction of the ball is pure physics, but golf is not only a physical-mechanical process of applying force to the ball. It is an inseparable interaction between the physical, physiological, and psychological qualities of the system. The aim of the golfer is not to achieve a hole in one. Good scores will follow as a consequence of good process. A perfect score, although welcome, is not the goal. However, if all is proper, if the golfer operates as a *whole in one,* the chances of the ball going to the target are more likely, and a hole in one is possible. If one worries about the score, then he or she will tend to react to the result of each shot as if that result were due to the take-away, weight transfer, swing path, planeclub face angle, etc. This can cause the golfer to overcompensate, reducing accuracy and consistency. Golfers need to guard against overdoing any one part of their swing.

If the golfer does not manage his or her system as a whole, performance will be poor, and the individual will be frustrated and angry. This, in turn, will most likely cause the person to try to overcompensate even more, which will further degrade performance. To focus on the parts without regard to the whole is to ignore what produces exceptional performance. The quality of the relationships between the parts makes the difference in the quality of overall performance.

Beyond Golf

Golfers do not have to interact with others during the process. People may play together, but normally they are more like a collection of individuals than an interdependent system. However, the golf game can be designed to create interdependence such as in Ryder Cup international play or a scramble format in local play. In team sports activities such as basketball, the nature of the interdependence between parts gives the game its unique character. Each player is like a specialized part of the body. The whole cannot perform without it, and the individual player has no purpose without the whole. The interaction between the players has to be orchestrated so that the parts can work together to optimize the performance of the whole.

The performing arts require the same kind of management of interactions within each individual artist and between individuals of the group, ie., the symphony orchestra, drama or company, etc. Just as performance of the golfer will degrade if one part of the body dominates the other parts, performance of the orchestra or chorus will be degraded if individuals play or sing louder or faster to gain attention for themselves, rather than doing what is appropriate to optimize their interactions with the other performers.

It is relatively easy to appreciate the fact that wholeness makes possible exceptional performance in golf and in the performing arts. It is not as easy to appreciate that this also is so in the rest of human enterprise.

We typically read, listen, and observe through our beliefs, presuppositions, and concepts. We act according to these mental models, just as a golfer's swing follows from his or her mental model of the right swing. Golfers cannot improve their game unless they learn an appropriate model and then practice, continually learning to apply that model until a better one comes along.

In order for golfers to avoid penalties for going out of bounds in the physical game, they may have to go beyond the boundaries of their mental model. This book asks that you do the same. The models and viewpoints presented in this book may be at odds with your present assumptions and ways of seeing things. If so, there is an opportunity to learn, but only if your present beliefs about what is appropriate, right, true, and practical do not get in the way of seeing alternatives.

The premise of this book is that human enterprise is more productive and rewarding for everyone when lived according to a whole-system view. This premise also pertains to the reading of this book. It is a system, a pattern of ideas. The individual ideas should make more sense after you have read the book in its entirety and the pattern has emerged.

I.

When Human Enterprise is a System

The way enterprises are conceptualized has a very large effect on what they do, and what they do affects the way they are conceptualized.

Russell Ackoff[1]

THERE IS A STORY about the stranger who challenged Picasso. "Why don't you paint things as they really are?" he asked. Picasso said he did not quite understand what the gentleman meant. The stranger produced from his wallet a photograph of his wife. "I mean, like that," he said. "That's how she is." Picasso coughed hesitantly and said, "She is rather small, isn't she? And somewhat flat?"[2]

Many years ago, Alfred Korzybski[3] made a distinction between mental maps, the symbolic language and structures we carry around in our heads, and the territory to which the maps refer. This is the foundation of the work of semanticists. It is why W. Edwards Deming[4] cautioned management that language had to be operationalized in order to do business. He warned that sellers and buyers can have the same understanding of the language of a contract or a product specification only when the statements refer to observable actions such as operations, tests, and procedures. There are many ways, for example, that the specification for a blanket, "must contain 50 percent wool," can be met in practice. Operationalization of the term, "50 percent wool," allows the words to have common meaning so that producers and consumers, sellers and buyers, will be able to agree that the specification has or has not been met. Misunderstandings and conflicts between people who do business together often are rooted in their failure to state in advance and in operational language how they will know when a commitment of one to the other has been fulfilled.

Abstractions are constructions *in* the mind, and *of* the mind. They have names such as: concept, mental model, assumption, belief, value, theory, idea, image, world view, paradigm. They influence our actions. They provide a ground for meaning, for interpretations of success and failure, for feelings of pride, joy, satisfaction, happiness, and sorrow. Although they greatly impact our lives, we often are not aware of them. The effects of hidden and unexamined assumptions in organizations, and methods to uncover them, is a subject of "learning organizations."[5]

Relevance of Mental Maps

Euclidean geometry is a mental construct, a way to think about and represent the physical world in two dimensions, as flat. Therefore a map of the Earth can be drawn on a piece of paper. However, we learned some time ago that the Earth is curved, not flat. A flat map does not accurately represent this curvature, and like any map of the Earth, it is not the same size as the territory it represents. This is an advantage, for if the map were exactly the same size as the territory, it would be a bit unwieldy to use; in fact, it would not be necessary.

Although the two-dimensional map has limits of application, it is still useful. It can work for some territories, such as construction of a building that covers such a small part of the Earth's surface that curvature is an insignificant factor to consider. It is much less useful–and can lead to great errors and costs–if used to construct a highway. Spherical geometry is a better map, but even spherical geometry has its limits as a map of the physical world. R. Buckminster Fuller[6] spent his life developing and applying an alternative geometry, a mental map that he felt was better aligned with the territory of the physical universe.

The capability of an enterprise to achieve its purpose depends a great deal on the applicability of management's mental map to the territory in which the enterprise operates. The territory is the external environment, which includes consumers, suppliers, and other people. It is also the enterprise itself, which includes human beings with their own aspirations, desires, inclinations, values; with their own maps.

There Is No Accounting for the Costs of Provincialism

The visible performance of an enterprise, the so-called bottom line, is produced by the activities of people. Yet, even though our enterprises are social systems, and transactions are between people, our models of accounting and performance management seem to apply more to the world of machines than to a world inhabited by conscious, thinking, reflecting, interacting, human beings. Dr. Deming told the controller of a large company that the visible costs that the financial system measured were trivial compared to the hidden costs. It quickly became obvious that this was not what the controller wanted to hear.

Figure 1, which is based on the experience of an automotive manufacturer a number of years ago, illustrates Dr. Deming's point.[7] The engine and transmission each had electronic components. An engineer found that a redesign of the engine components would eliminate the need for electronic components on the transmission and save $80, but would require adding $30 to the cost of the engine. The management of the division that manufactured the engine rejected the proposal. Since they operated as a profit center, they would be penalized for adding cost. Their job was to reduce the cost of manufacturing an engine, not the cost of manufacturing a vehicle. What incredible suboptimization! The company manufactured one million units per year; therefore the unrealized annual savings was $50 million. Since the company was producing a return on investment (ROI) of five percent, it would require an investment of one billion dollars to earn this amount!

	Engine	Transmission	Both
Present cost	$100	$80	$180
Proposed cost	$130	$0	$130
Proposed savings per unit			$50
Proposed annual savings			$50,000,000

Figure 1. Cost of powertrain electronic components

There are similar examples in all sorts of other enterprises. I encountered a situation in which the customer service department needed to replace a twenty-year-old vehicle. However, since the cost of a new vehicle would have been charged to their budget and a complete overhaul of the old vehicle would have been charged to the budget of the maintenance department, they chose to have the vehicle overhauled–at greater cost than replacement!

What Cost Accounting Misses

The costs incurred by failure to consider the effects of one's plans and actions on other parts of the enterprise reflect the widely-held assumption that the performance of the whole is the simple sum of the performance of each of the parts considered separately. Consequently, each individual person and unit is urged to do their best so that the whole will become its best.

Figure 2 illustrates the calculation of performance expected under the traditional assumption that the whole will be its best if the individual units do their best. This is

(1) Manager	(2) Expected Results	(3) Actual Results
(2) Purchasing	+	–
(3) Engineering	+	–
(4) Assembly	+	+
(5) Overall Results	+3	–1

Figure 2. Performance under traditional assumptions: the whole is the sum of the parts, each separately doing its best

shown for three interdependent organizations: Purchasing, Product Engineering, and the Assembly plant. Typically, each unit, or department, independently establishes plans and objectives that will satisfy the global goals or objectives of a higher-level manager. Objectives usually are quantified. Each unit plans to accomplish the local objective for itself, as indicated by the + in column 2, rows 2, 3, and 4 (see Figure 2). The + indicates positive performance, e.g., dollars of revenue, sales volume, or cost reduction. The plans, which are expectations of performance, are aggregated up the management hierarchy into the overall objective of the senior manager of the function or business unit. Throughout the year management compares actual performance to plan, e.g., the budget. Negative deviations (variances) are discussed and corrective actions are taken. Each manager is rated at the end of the year according to department performance, and rewarded or punished accordingly.

There is an assumption implicit in this method that each individual has control over the performance for which he or she is held responsible. Therefore, if one were doing one's best, working hard, one would succeed. The problem is that attempts to meet local objectives and maximize local performance may very well produce actual performance that is worse than one would expect by adding up the separate plans.

Figure 2, column 3 shows not only that actual results were less than expected, but that there was an overall loss, even though each department planned and acted to produce positive results. The reason for this can be seen in Figure 3, which expands Figure 2 to show the effects of unplanned interactions between units. (The results in Figure 3, row 5 are the same as in Figure 2, column 3.) This may help to explain how senior management can be promised, say, a 15 percent gain from each unit, but at the end of the year receive much less, perhaps even a loss. This paradox results from traditional assumptions and methods that hide the source of gains, costs, and losses.

Figure 3 shows that overall performance suffers when individual departments work to optimize their own performance locally and do not work together to optimize the performance of the whole system. The independent plans and actions of each department, are shown in column 1, rows 2, 3, and 4. Each department influences results in the following ways:

1. Influences its own performance. The effects are shown in the shaded cells. Each department has

(1) Department actions	(2) Effects on Puchasing	(3) Effects on Engineering	(4) Effects on Assembly	(5) Effects on Whole System
(2) Purchasing: Sources to supplier with lowest price, but no engineering capability.	+ Reduces expenditures by 10%.	– Hires engineer to work with supplier, Purchasing, and Assembly to solve problems.	– Parts unusable or hard to assemble. Can't meet production schedules.	–1
(3) Product Engineering: Redesigns product and replaces many individual parts with fewer subassemblies.	– Purchasing spends much time with Engineering to help supplier produce subassemblies.	+ Higher quality and reliability, better appearance.	+ Fewer product parts have less variability. Easier and faster to assemble than previous design.	+1
(4) Assembly: Retools assembly process for new product design.	– Supplier's parts cause problems in assembly process. Buyer "lives" in plant.	– Engineering spends much time in plant with supplier and buyer.	+ Faster to assemble product. Lower labor costs.	–1
(5) Results Attributed to Departments	–1	–1	+1	–1

Figure 3. Attempts to maximize local performance can lower overall performance and everyone can lose

developed plans and acted to produce a + for itself. These results also are shown in Figure 2, column 2, where an overall result of +3 is expected:

Purchasing (Figure 3, row 2, column 1), in order to meet cost reduction objectives, sourced one of the subassemblies to a supplier with the lowest price, even though the supplier had no engineering capability. This helped Purchasing save 10 percent in expenditures for purchased parts. It gets a + for itself (row 2, column 2).

Product Engineering (row 3, column 1) redesigned the product to replace many individual parts with fewer, more complex assemblies. It gets a + for itself (row 3, column 3) because the new design improved overall product quality, reliability, and appearance.

Assembly (row 4, column 1) retooled to assemble the larger subassemblies. It replaced some workers with robots to speed up the process and reduce labor costs. It gets a + for itself (row 4, column 4).

2. Influences performance of other departments, and they, in turn, affect it. These interaction effects are shown in the non-shaded cells of rows 2, 3, and 4 in columns 2, 3, and 4. For example:

   Purchasing (row 2) negatively affected Product Engineering (row 2, column 3), since the lack of supplier engineering capability made it necessary for Engineering to hire an engineer to work with the supplier. Purchasing also negatively impacted Assembly (row 2, column 4). Both of these effects, in turn, negatively impacted Purchasing, since it now had to spend more time in meetings with Engineering (row 3, column 2). Purchasing also had to send a buyer to "live" in the supplier's plant (row 4, column 2).

   The effects of one department on another may be positive. The redesigned product was easier

> to assemble (row 3, column 4), although this gain was offset by the poor quality subassemblies that the plant received (row 2, column 4).
>
> The totals in row 5, columns 2, 3, and 4, show the results that would be attributed to each department. Purchasing, for example, appears to produce a negative result (row 5, column 2). The purchasing manager would be held accountable for this result, even though performance of the department was negatively impacted by interactions with Engineering (row 3, column 2) and Assembly (row 4, column 2). The result (row 5, column 2) will form the basis of performance feedback and evaluation of the purchasing manager.
>
> The effects of each department on the system are shown in column 5. Purchasing (row 2, column 5) and Assembly (row 4, column 5) each caused a loss to the system, even though they met their own local objectives (shown in shaded cells). Product Engineering produced an overall positive effect on the system (row 3, column 5). Overall, the interactions between departments produced a loss. The bottom line is negative. The attempt to separately optimize each department suboptimized the system as a whole.

The visible results include the results produced by the interactions, but the effects of the interactions are invisible to the management system. Results produced by any department alone, or any individual alone, and those produced by interactions with other parts of the system, are confounded and cannot practically be separated. Most performance evaluation methods, however, are based on the assumption that performance is produced and controllable where it appears. Interaction effects are not considered.

The assumption of independence that underlies traditional approaches to cost accounting, management by objectives, planning, and budgeting makes it very difficult to predict global results because it ignores the effects of interactions between local parts of the system. Moreover, the process of periodically reviewing local performance throughout the year and trying to compensate for negative variances can increase the variability of the system as a whole. Individuals overcompensate when they think they will not meet their local targets (just as in golf). They respond to nearly every deviation from target as if it had an identifiable and locally correctable cause, and do not consider the possibility of interactions with other parts of the system or of variations due to chance. Local overcompensation produces problems for people in other parts of the system. Performance of the enterprise could be improved dramatically if it learned to operate as *one whole system.*

A System Is a Map

A *system* is a map, an abstraction of the territory, not the territory itself. It is the way we think about the territory, about "what's out there," although "what's out there," and what's in our mind cannot easily be separated, if at all. We know a system by the map we use to describe it. There are objects and events that we see and hear, but our mind makes the connections; the *eye of the mind* either sees or fails to see certain kinds of relationships between the parts. The territory is not the words and pictures used to describe it, and it is certainly not a description in the mind of any single individual.

A System Operates over Time and Place

We cannot see the whole system at once, since it is spread over various places and operates over time. The state of the system, therefore, can't be evaluated at any point-in-time, or in any one locality, even though various methods of evaluation try to do that (see Figure 3). Interdependencies, and therefore the need to manage interactions, are not always obvious because actions and consequences may be widely separated in time and place. Enterprises are human-social systems. Human memory causes a social system to have expectations and goals that are influenced by what has happened in the past and what people want to happen in the future.

A System Is Not a Collection; System Means Interdependence

A group may be called a "team," but in fact may perform more like a collection of parts than an interdependent, interacting system. This can be seen when exceptional athletes from various teams are brought together to form a team for a unique event like an All-Star game or Olympic competition. Overall performance is not as good as one would expect, given the talents of the individuals. The players have difficulty blending and flowing together as one whole. Professional musicians may observe that when superstar soloists get together to play chamber music, they give a good performance, but they are not as deeply integrated as an established group such as string quartet, piano duo, etc.

Failure to understand the principle that performance depends on how well interdependent parts fit together can lead to unsolved mysteries, wrong conclusions, and a waste of time. In the mid 1980s, a Japanese automotive manufacturer was producing cars with much higher levels of customer satisfaction than its American competitor. The American company tried to understand why this was so. The Americans analyzed the Japanese vehicle and their own vehicle by the following process: (a) each vehicle was completely disassembled; (b) specialists examined the parts, e.g., the engine engineers examined the engines, the body engineers examined the body panels, the chassis engineers examined the steering and suspension; (c) the specialists wrote up their findings, which were submitted to an engineering manager, who combined the separate reports.

The results were puzzling. Part for part, the American car appeared to be better than the Japanese car, e.g., thicker gauge steel for the body panels. Why the puzzle? The method of *analysis* failed to get at the holistic experience of customers. Customers did not buy a collection of parts, they bought a whole system–and that is what they evaluated. In their eyes, the experience of high quality was due to the way everything fit together, the way the parts of the vehicle interacted with each other and with themselves as customers, e.g., comfort and convenience of seats and controls, smoothness of the engine and shifting of the transmission, to produce the customer's whole experience.

The method of analysis of the American company–the independent actions of the specialists, the aggregation of the data by a manager–followed the same map, same model as the method used to design the vehicle. Every part met engineering specifications, every individual was doing his and her best, yet the vehicle as a whole did not have the expected quality. The American vehicle did not perform as a whole system in the eyes of customers, because the people who designed and built it did not perform as a whole system.

Systems Are Contained within Systems

A system, by definition, is an integrated whole. Yet, a whole cannot live by itself. It is a part of a larger whole–a pattern of relationships–that sustains it and provides the purpose for its existence. Each part of a human being–eye, hand, heart, kidney, etc.–is itself a system whose functioning maintains and sustains the life of the larger system, the human being, in which it is contained. Yet, each part of the body could not survive without the whole that it serves. Each whole human being could not live without the functions provided by the various parts (subsystems) of its body; nor could the individual survive without the sustenance provided by the larger biological-social-economic ecology (suprasystem) of which it is a part.

The quality of the life of any whole depends on the quality of the relationships between the parts it contains and sustains, e.g., cooperation between the parts of the body to produce a golf swing, cooperation between people in an enterprise to serve the purpose of that whole, cooperation between enterprises to serve the larger economy. If an enterprise did not serve the purposes of customers in the "market" (a suprasystem, which is a useful abstraction in our minds), it would not exist for long as a whole body. The corporation would become a corpse. Healthy living is

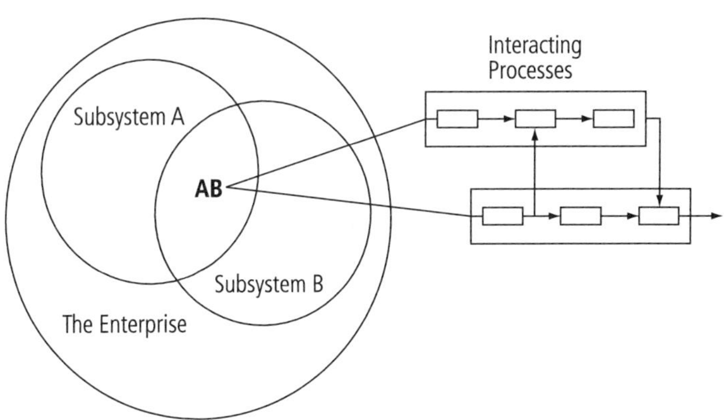

Figure 4. ***The enterprise contains interacting wholes (subsystems)***

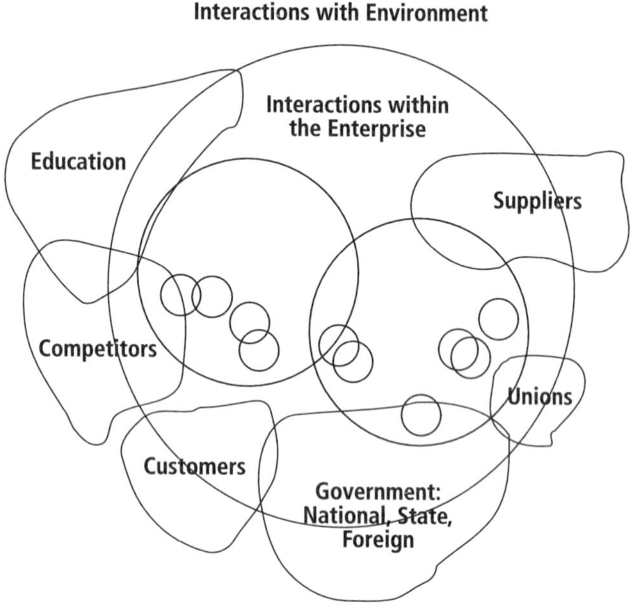

Figure 5. The enterprise interacts with other systems in its containing whole (suprasystem)

a dynamic process of continual interaction. Relationships help to create the character and capability of an individual, and an enterprise.

Figure 4 illustrates the enterprise as a whole that is composed of interacting systems (subsystems of the enterprise). Figure 5 shows the enterprise as a system contained within a larger social-economic system (suprasystem). This map is one of many ways to think about the enterprise as a system, but it has limitations, as do all maps. It does not capture the dynamic, interactive nature of a system.

A system is more complex than can be represented on paper. Since a system cannot be represented adequately by the viewpoint of one person, a map that synthesizes the views of others in the system will enrich everyone's image of the whole. Seeing the whole is a continual process of minds interacting.

The Whole Emerges through Interaction of its Parts

The capabilities and properties of a whole, unlike a collection, cannot be predicted by adding the characteristics of the component parts taken separately. "The whole is greater than the sum of the parts," means that new characteristics and new behaviors emerge in the containing system that are not present in any of its contained parts. This is the outcome of the arrangement, the relationships, the interactions of the parts. One might say that the whole *transcends* its parts, and yet, at the same time, the character and capability of the whole is *immanent* in the relationships between the parts that give rise to the performance of that whole.

Consider six 12" x 12" squares of wood, each 1" thick. Not one of them has the capability of containment, yet if one fits them together to form a box, the box has the property of containment. A new property emerged from the *interaction* of the parts. Consider piles of bricks, lumber, and other materials on an empty lot. Architects, tradespeople, and others interact (well or poorly) to transform the collection of parts into a house. The house is a system with different properties than its parts, and it is a dynamic system because of the ongoing exchange of information between the parts that maintains a stable internal climate (as long as people don't keep adjusting the thermostat), in the face of a variable, and perhaps turbulent, external environment. Such a property cannot be found in the furnace itself, in any of the parts of the furnace looked at separately, or in any of the other parts of the house looked at individually.

Human Relationships that Fit: The Economics of Cooperation

Optimization is a process of working to achieve the full capability inherent in the whole enterprise by blending the talents and knowledge of people. Figure 6 (in contrast to Figure 3) shows how loss can be minimized and enterprise performance can be optimized when people have the information they need and are willing to cooperate for the good of the enterprise as a whole.

The partners in the relationship plan together to optimize the larger system that contains them. This may mean that one or more of the parties may have to incur what traditionally may appear to be a loss. In Figure 6, we see that Purchasing (row 2, column 1) and Assembly (row 4, column 1) each selected actions that would affect themselves negatively in the short-term (shaded cells of rows 2 and 4) in order to enable the whole enterprise to do better. The end result is optimization of the whole system, which produces a gain of +6 (row 5, column 5). This contributes

(1) Department actions	(2) Effects on Puchasing	(3) Effects on Engineering	(4) Effects on Assembly	(5) Effects on Whole System
(2) Purchasing: Selects new supplier able to engineer and produce subassemblies.	– Higher piece price includes amortization of supplier engineering capability.	++ Lower cost to engineer subassembly.	+ Better quality parts make assembly easier and faster.	+2
(3) Product Engineering: Redesigns product replacing many small parts with fewer subassemblies.	+ Fewer parts to purchase, fewer suppliers to work with, less problems to solve.	+ Longer-lasting design. Fewer revisions needed.	+ Fewer parts to assemble, fewer part #'s to receive & track, less total variability, better fit.	+3
(4) Assembly: Retools process for subassembly parts and just-in-time (JIT) delivery.	+ JIT delivery reduces supplier inventory cost; piece price is reduced.	+ Engineers spend time improving design for better assembly rather than solving problems.	– Incremental cost incurred to retool for larger subassemblies and JIT delivery.	+1
(5) Overall Results	+1	+4	+1	+6
(6) Credit Given to Departments	+2	+2	+2	+6

Figure 6.* *Cooperation optimizes enterprise performance and everyone can win

to profit and can be used to develop new products and services, improve existing ones, and reinvest in the enterprise in other ways.

Financial results also may be shared, but it would not be logical to try to identify the separate contribution of system participants. Purchasing and Assembly intentionally have added cost or otherwise taken a loss locally to help the system, while Product Engineering has shown a gain because of this. Since all departments are interacting and inseparable parts of the system, they share the credit equally for the total results (row 6). This follows from the same principle that we applied to the performance of the golfer: The various components of the body cannot be individually credited for their contribution to a good swing. Failure to equitably recognize contributions to performance not only violates system logic, but also demoralizes individuals and creates internal competition that will jeopardize the cooperation needed to continue to perform in an optimal manner.

Equity in profit sharing doesn't mean that there are not differences in salary for engineers, buyers, and other system participants. Salary is determined by factors such as market rate, level of education, seniority, experience, and knowledge. Salary increases should be kept separate from recognition and performance feedback.[8]

If profit sharing is used, it has to be managed in a way that does not create a dependence on extrinsic incentives, nor degrade the contribution that people make because they believe it is intrinsically right to help the enterprise and to provide something of value to society.

Competitors Are a Part of the System

When the system is optimized, there is greater gain for all; everyone can win. This logic extends to relationships between competitors. Dr. Deming observed that a poor competitor can hurt you as well as himself, can ruin your name as well as his own. When one company, for example, offers the customer price rebates in order to stimulate sales, competitors are pressured by their own sales organizations, who are driven by market share, to do the same.

When everyone is offering rebates, sales and market share of each company will eventually average out to their previous levels, since rebates no longer differentiate products.

Customers may think (although not systemically) that lower prices are great, but eventually they also can lose. Price wars reduce profits of all the competitors. Lower profits may increase the cost of borrowing. When the price war ends, companies may raise their prices to make up for lost profits and to recover their increased costs. This can further reduce sales and profit. All of this results in less funds available to develop new products and services, and customers will have fewer choices in the future. The competitors, in the heat of battle, also may bad-mouth each other. This can cause consumers to lose confidence in the products and services of all of the companies and seek alternatives, if possible. In the long run, no one in the system wins, unless an upstart competitor sneaks in with innovative alternative products and services while the others are fighting it out.

II.

When Human Enterprise is a Social Ecology

Without an aim, there is no system. The aim of the system must be clear to everyone in the system.

W. Edwards Deming[9]

Our business and economic organizations should be viewed as life systems.

H. Thomas Johnson[10]

"SYSTEM THINKING" spread throughout the business, education, and government communities in the 1990s. Yet there are many ways to think about a system, many maps one can draw. What system characteristics and principles can help the enterprise *live* successfully? Machines also are systems, ones that operate according to the principles discovered by Isaac Newton. Command and control structures are good for managing systems of machines because machines operate according to linear cause and effect: apply an external force, feed in other materials and other inputs, and see the results (outputs). If you don't like the results, change the inputs. The machines don't reflect on their situation, don't have aspirations, don't have better ideas. The big problem for enterprise occurs when human beings are managed as machines, or as replaceable parts of machines, without minds, feelings, or motives of their own. They are treated as if they also need an external force to energize and direct them.

Many organizations, even those that claim to be team oriented, are managed according to this mental model of enterprise-as-machine. This is revealed by the language and metaphors that people use, e.g., "well-oiled machine," or "shift gears." What expectations do such images create in others? What actions and performance do they produce? What would be the difference in capability if management thought about the enterprise not as a mechanical-physical system, but as a system of human beings, a social ecology with common and individual purposes?

The management mental model of the enterprise as machine-like still prevails; therefore so does top-down command and control. This became evident when *re-engineering*–which was essentially a method to achieve short-term cost reductions by removing parts of the system, especially the people–began to spread rapidly throughout business organizations in the early 1990s. These methods appealed to some managers, I believe, because they were not that far removed from Frederick Taylor's mechanistic industrial engineering and therefore did not require managers to change their thinking; it fit in with their current paradigm of management.

Years ago, a "friend" who thought he was a mechanic, as did I, offered to improve my car's performance by "fixing" the engine. He disassembled the engine, fiddled around with the parts, and reassembled it. Some parts were left over. He said that they were not needed and did not know why these "extra" parts were put there in the first place. The car ran better than before, for a short while, then it died suddenly. Any business can make performance look better today by eliminating some of its parts and reducing costs today, but what about tomorrow? One large business that was losing money reduced the number of employees by 30 percent in order to lower costs. When this actually made things worse and losses increased, the company decided to remove larger parts of the system and began to sell off some of its business units to raise cash, thereby accelerating the process of self-destruction.

Management should be moving the enterprise in a direction away from the stifling effects of the kinds of mechanistic thinking reflected in methods such as re-engineering, and toward "de-engineering," as Margaret Wheatley[11] calls it. Russell Ackoff[12] observes that when an organization is conceptualized as a machine, management considers the purposes of people to be irrelevant to the way the people are managed and the way the enterprise behaves. This inhibits effective adaptation of the enterprise in turbulent, chaotic, unpredictable environments. However, when enterprises are conceptualized and managed as social systems, and individuals have the kinds of freedom of conscious and purposeful choice that they are able to responsibly exercise in the larger democratic society, the enterprise will be much more able to act effectively. It will have a greater capability to respond *(passively adapt)* to unpredictable environmental changes that already have occurred, as well as the ability to innovate and shape the external environment *(actively adapt)*. Such an organization is better able to perceive opportunities and take advantage of them.

Lessons from Systems Behaving Naturally

What system principles, what organizational arrangements would better enable the enterprise to maintain resilience and flexibility in a rapidly changing world? Gregory Bateson[13] asked us to learn from the natural world, to let nature teach us, to think as nature thinks. What useful lessons can management learn from the ecologically sound functioning of natural systems?

Wheatley[14] offers enterprise models from quantum physics (not the Newtonian physics of mechanical systems) and molecular biology. Order and pattern are created, not by externally imposed structures (e.g., command and control organization charts that define relationships vertically) and complex controls, but through guiding principles inherent in the natural processes that allow the autonomous interaction of the individual parts of the system.

Michael Rothschild argues throughout his book, *Bionomics: Economy as Ecosystem,* that the natural ecological systems of the biological world, such as a rain forest with the interdependencies and adaptation capabilities of the life contained within it, offer a better way to think about the dynamics of human interactions in a free market economy than do the Newtonian laws of the physical world. Life in natural ecological systems functions and survives, not through predictable sequences of cause and effect processes, but rather through the dynamic, interactive exchange of information that enables organisms to regulate themselves in the context of what is happening around them. This self-regulation occurs within the system, not from outside of it. Organisms in a rain forest are in a continual process of growth and adjustment. A free market economy functions in the same way. A spontaneous order emerges, not from central planning, but from the interactions of self-interested buyers and sellers who adjust to shifting prices and other changes in the environment. Individuals cooperate because it is in their best interests to do so.

The fact that the principles of a free market economy seem to align with the understanding of biologists about the way ecosystems work is more than coincidence. Rothschild[15] notes that Darwin studied economics, including Adam Smith's book, *The Wealth of Nations,* prior to formulation of his theory of natural selection. Darwin learned that a viable economy was possible because of the wide variation in the talents, inclinations, and interests of people. Individuals can earn a living by using their special talents to produce goods and services that they sell or trade for goods and services that they can't produce. A viable economic system is a continual interaction between consumers and producers. If there is no demand for one's products or services, the associated skills, knowledge, and technology are replaced by those in greater demand. Over time, the character of the system as a whole changes. It is a self-selecting, self-regulating process.

Whole in a Whole

Darwin may have had Adam Smith's ideas in mind during his observations in the Galapagos Islands, but both Smith and Darwin did not think ecologically. Bateson[16] writes that Darwin looked at the survival of single individuals, or groups of individuals such as a family unit. He did not consider the relationship between the individual and the environment. In order to understand what is going on, one cannot look only at the individual; rather, one has to look at the system as a whole and see the individual-within-its-environment. The unit of survival is a whole within a whole. This gets to the heart of the argument made in Chapter 1 that the contributions of the individual and the system are inseparable.

Fritjof Capra[17] makes a similar point when he compares *holistic* and *ecological* views. A holistic view of, say, a bicycle (his example), enables one to see the bicycle as a functional whole and to understand the interaction of its parts accordingly. An ecological view considers, in addition, how the bicycle is embedded in its natural and social environment: where the raw materials that went into it came from, how it was manufactured, how its use affects the natural environment and the community which uses it, and so on.

Adam Smith[18] believed that when people pursue their own interests, both they and the society benefit. He felt that individuals led by an "invisible hand" often promote the interest of society, even though that is not their intention, and perhaps contribute even more than when they intend to promote the public good directly. But in today's highly interdependent social-environmental ecology, where local actions can have dramatic global effects, which in turn have local consequences, what does it mean to act in one's self interest? How can one know whether one's actions today will not eventually harm the sustaining natural social-economic ecology and hence come back to harm the individual tomorrow? It seems to me that self-interest can be achieved only when the individual behaves according to the guiding principle that one's own health and well-being is intertwined and inseparable from the health and well-being of the containing whole. If the whole ecology does not survive, the individuals within it will not survive.

Adam Smith's "invisible hand," according to Capra,[19] is a metaphor that describes the self-regulatory processes in social life. But the invisible hand cannot function effectively unless individuals have relevant information to evaluate the potential consequences of their actions. This can come through cooperation. Rothschild[20], looking at the economy as a whole, writes that mutually beneficial relationships, common among species in nature, can lead to mutual profitability in business. However, this viewpoint is at odds with the popular notion, erroneous yet eagerly applied in almost every type of enterprise, that in the natural world competition pits species against species to assure "survival of the fittest." Alfie Kohn.[21] influenced by the thinking of Stephen Jay Gould,[22] presents evidence that natural selection occurs without any discernable struggle and that competition actually discourages survival. Survival in nature is more likely when individuals of the same or different species, work with, rather than against, each other.

The Enterprise-in-the-Individual

People work within an enterprise, and at the same time the enterprise works within the minds and hearts of the people within it. Command and control hierarchies and their systems of management make it very difficult for people to treat each other as if they were intellectual and spiritual whole human beings. The decoupling of human beings at work from their wholeness as human beings was institutionalized in business in the early 1900s through the industrial engineering methods of Frederick Taylor. In order to maximize the speed and efficiency of production, work was broken into simple, repetitive tasks. Parts of people produced parts of products. People did not understand how they fit into the larger picture. Some people on the assembly line who screwed parts together all day long may have gotten the idea that the company was in the screw-tightening business.

The management mental model of the place of human beings in the enterprise that Taylor introduced early in the twentieth century still exists today, and not only on factory production lines, or on service production lines, or in repetitive office work.[23] This can occur in the offices of lawyers and accountants, in the administration of hospitals and schools–anywhere. It is found wherever human beings are demeaned by management reliance on extrinsic rewards and punishments, such as financial incentives, and awards, such as "employee of the month" or "team of the month," to get people to do what management wants them to do. When the management system relies on bribes and punishments, it encourages individuals, or teams, to behave in competitive, self-optimizing, self-protective ways.[24] They do what is necessary to win rewards and avoid losses. People are denied the opportunity to develop a sense of responsibility to others and to the organization and its purposes. The use of extrinsic forces to push people (as one applies force to push a rock or other inert object) has other costs. Managers must spend the time to administer rewards and punishments, as well as monitor and inspect people to assure that they are conforming in the prescribed ways.

Why is it that people enjoy activities outside of work that do not seem very different from their activities at work (which they find unpleasant)? Golf, to continue an example, could be viewed as work, except that one starts the day with enthusiasm, enjoys working, even when the weather is bad, and gladly pays to do it. Why is it that work is work and golf is play? Would golf be fun if the boss came along, set scoring objectives, frequently measured results, and admonished everyone to do better? How many individuals who are unhappy with their jobs derive great satisfaction from restoring cars, woodworking, or other hobbies that require the same skills and knowledge used at work? Why do people who dislike their jobs in the office voluntarily contribute their knowledge and time to civic or church activities? Why shouldn't work be enjoyable? Why can't it be fun? Why are work and play treated as mutually exclusive? Why do we call it "work," a word that means to expend energy in order to remove obstacles and connotes travail, pain and suffering, toil and drudgery?

The Individual-in-the-Enterprise

Most leaders of business enterprises believe that it is beneficial to both consumers and to enterprise to be able to operate in the marketplace without government constraints that prevent businesses from working together. Why shouldn't the same principles of freedom and flexibility also work within the enterprise? How to reconcile the freedoms and rights of conscious, purposeful human beings with the needs of the larger social system is a perennial and profound problem of leadership. Plato struggled with this twenty-four hundred years ago in *The Republic.*

The motives, standards, and behaviors found in communities of professionals may provide some ideas about how a system of cooperation might work within an enterprise of free people. It already exists to a small extent when people from different companies work together in industry and professional associations for everyone's benefit. Michael Polanyi[25] wrote that a free society works best when individuals are able to choose to cooperate with other individuals in order to pursue ends that all deem worthy. This is especially evident in the behavior of professionals such as scientists, judges, clergy, artists, writers, journalists, philosophers, historians, and economists. They associate with others in their field in order to achieve personal aims, yet each is part of the same whole because everyone accepts the same professional and ethical standards and recognizes the same precedent and tradition.

There is no central control, yet a *spontaneous ordered whole* emerges from the continual interactions of people. There is a system of control; it is one of *mutual adjustments* and *mutual authority*. Science, for example, has made tremendous progress operating in this manner. Scientists influence each other through their sharing of information and facts. One's authority comes from the respect one is given by colleagues for his or her knowledge. Scientists tend to work with others in closely related fields, but science as a whole is a system of *overlapping neighborhoods*.

According to Polanyi, the inner, private motives of individuals prod them into these systems of spontaneous social order, but the motive that moves them into the appropriate relationships with one another comes from the common understanding within the profession of their duties and obligations. Therefore, regardless of the private motives that move a person to be, for example, a judge–

ambition for status, power, respect, money–one is not a judge unless one performs according to the activities and obligations that constitute being a judge. Judges are therefore "motivated" to find the relevant law and the relevant facts and to make a decision that either follows the precedents or creates a new precedent on grounds that one's colleagues can, or ought to, find reasonable.

III.

Leading the Enterprise in Concert

An example of a system, well optimized, is a good orchestra. The players are not there to play solos as prima donnas, each one trying to catch the ear of the listener. They are there to support each other. Individually they need not be the best players in the country . . . An orchestra is judged by listeners, not so much by illustrious players, but by the way they work together. The conductor, as manager, begets cooperation between players, as a system, every player to support the others. There are other aims for an orchestra, such as joy in work for the players and for the conductor.

W. Edwards Deming[26]

IMAGINE A LIVE PERFORMANCE of a symphony orchestra where the strings are in Chicago, the winds are in New York, the percussion section is in Washington D.C., and the customers are in Los Angeles, Seattle, and Boston. This is one problem performing arts enterprises do not have to face. The performers and the theater audience are in the same place. In other kinds of enterprises, members of the "cast," or "company," often are located in different places–different floors in the same building, different buildings in the same area, or different areas throughout the country and the world. Customers may be even more disbursed. It may be inconvenient when performers are spread out over different locations, but not much of a problem with electronic communication (although face-to-face communication is richer). The vital challenge to enterprise is how to orchestrate the performers into one whole system.

Successful performing arts enterprises perform in accordance with whole-system principles. They can provide a living model for other kinds of human enterprise. If businesses, especially those that produce goods, viewed themselves as a continual live performance–which actually they are–then it would be much easier for them to see when they do not work in harmony. Failure to behave as a whole system cannot be hidden behind numbers or compensated for by costly inspection and rework.

Many of the words that the performing arts use connote whole system relationships. *Harmonious* means that the parts are agreeably related, that is, they are characterized by accord in sentiment or action. Harmony is a means of joining, of fitting things together such as when notes are combined in an aesthetically pleasing manner to produce a chord. *Chord* is a short version of *accord. Concert,* the verb, comes from the Latin roots *com,* or with, and *certare,* to strive, hence, "to act together in cooperation, to bring into agreement."

Performing artists are able see how their role or function contributes to the whole performance. They know what business they are in. What would be the quality of an orchestral performance if the musicians decided to play whenever and however they wanted? What would be the effect if one or two musicians were removed from each section in order to re-engineer the process, or if the conductor directed all musicians to play at the same time in order to raise efficiency? There would be maximum efficiency with zero quality. There would be no whole, no product, just noise. The performance would have nothing at all to do with the purpose of the enterprise and its customers.

When the performers are connected optimally, together they have a capability to produce a whole product and service that no one of them can produce. The artists act *in concert,* in harmony with themselves (each one tries to play as technically perfect as they can) and with each other. They join together, united by purpose into a whole that is one intelligence, one consciousness, one mind, one heart. (The Latin origin of *accord* meant "heart-to-heart.")

Leadership that Connects

Art, as in *artisan,* originally referred to the skill needed to join things together. The role of leader in a social ecology is to connect the artists into a pattern that is able to perform in concert. Without this joining together, the performing arts enterprise could not perform; it could not live. Wholeness is inherent in its existence.

In the theater or concert hall, artists interpret the plan–script or musical score–without worrying that an outside disturbance might interfere with the artistic performance. In other kinds of enterprise, especially business, people need to be in a state of readiness to face changes in the environment, e.g., from government legislation, from competitors, from failures anywhere in the world economy, which sometimes occur overnight. A jazz group, therefore, might be a better model than a symphony orchestra, since jazz musicians have more freedom to improvise around the theme or purpose of a piece.

Max DePree, former Chairman of Herman Miller, Inc., in his book, *Leadership Jazz,* describes the concepts that guided him in his leadership role of orchestrating human expression. He asks leaders to "think of achievement as a collaborative and synthetic result," and to recognize that most of a leader's work "depends heavily on the quality of our relationships."[27] He writes: "An organization's cultural harmony is fragile. I'm talking about the sweet music that emanates from diverse and productive groups of people. Leaders certainly have a hand in creating the atmosphere where this kind of harmony can exist, but they don't direct it or mandate it or control it."[28] Jazz-band leaders know how to integrate the "voices" in the band without diminishing their uniqueness.[29]

Unlike DePree, some managers believe that abandonment of tight hierarchical control can only lead to chaos. They see any alternative to top-down control as laissez faire management, and therefore an abdication by management of its responsibility to maintain order. Yet control absolutely exists in the performing arts. It may be obvious, as when the conductor stands on the podium in front of the orchestra, or it may be subtle, as when the function of conductor, or leader, resides not in a single individual, but in the interactions that create the whole. This can be seen in a jazz or a string quartet, or in a chamber orchestra with 30 musicians. Whether the function of leading and conducting is visible or invisible, control comes from within, very much in the manner of mutual adjustment that characterizes the performance of other professionals.

There is another orchestration role or function that operates in drama or opera. The cast member who helps to make the plot work, who helps the action unfold toward its purpose or intended outcome, is called the *Fifth Business*.[30] This individual is one of the actors, a part of the drama, but not in the spotlight. There are individuals in various enterprises who play this role. They are almost invisible, but they can be recognized when people say, "I don't know what she does, but when she's around everything seems to go better." That person is in the Fifth Business. She helps people to more fully express their individual talents and to connect with each other so that the performance can come to life. Such a person does not seek credit; it is not in their nature. Seeking credit is incompatible with the role; the person must stay in the background to be effective. This role is similar to that of "servant leader."[31]

The performing arts validate the ecological principle that individual freedom, guided by responsibility *to* others (not *for* others), leads not to chaos, but to creative order of the whole. Peter B. Vaill writes in *Managing as a Performing Art*[32] that the performing arts provide a framework to appropriately discipline the creativity and personal expression of each performer both during solos, which are performed within a system of support from others, and during ensemble parts when everyone is playing or performing together.

Practice Is Necessary, but Doesn't Make Perfect

Practice is required, but it doesn't make perfect in the performing arts, or in other types of enterprise, since there is no state of perfection. Models can be improved and better ones can be found. The artists can practice individually and rehearse together before the performance. Performing artists work continually to approximate an ideal of professional excellence, in collaboration and by themselves. Optimal interaction is an ideal to work toward but never can be achieved. Unlike the stable environment of the concert hall or theater where artists perform, many surprises occur in the "theater of action" of a business. In order to precisely optimize, one would have to know the state of the external world, e.g., the marketplace, consumer preferences, and all of the plans and actions that exist within the enterprise. Operationally, this cannot be accomplished in a continually changing external and internal environment.

There is another reason. The business is performing continuously. This makes it impossible before the performance to practice interacting–there is no "before," there is always "during." People are continuously rehearsing for future actions, future adjustments. Planning is a part of this rehearsal. In an ecologically-minded system, planning is not done by an outside agency such as a central planning department; it is done by the performers themselves.

Whole individuals plan for the whole in which they will act. Planning helps people to expand their mental model to encompass more of the ecosystem, and thereby learn how they can better support each other. In the following chapters, some methods are discussed that have helped people gain an *ecological* (outward to the suprasystem) and a *holistic* (inward to subsystems) understanding so that they can interact in mutually supportive ways. They have applied the principle seen on car bumper stickers, "Think Globally, Act Locally," although I would change it to "Think Globally, Interact Locally, Make Adjustments."

Scoring without Numbers: Enterprise Can't Live by Figures Alone

In business, one typically thinks of *scoring* as producing or recording a number, a result. Management typically uses figures every day to evaluate whether the enterprise is on course toward its objectives. Scoring in the performing arts is to orchestrate, to arrange or combine the parts in an optimal manner. It also enables prediction, but without numerical measurement. A score in the performing arts is a model that arranges the parts of the performance into a coherent whole, much like the model of a golfer's swing. The golfer follows the model; the orchestra follows the score. A good model, or score, will produce the desired results (with variation) when it is well executed.

The ecological question is how to provide valid information (feedback) to help individuals regulate themselves and mutually adjust their interactions. An individual performer or group–in music or sports or business–may consistently play poorly under one set of conditions, and well in another. Is it the instruments, or the venue, or the performers? Why is performance as it is, and how can it be improved? We saw in Chapter 1 how interactions are confounded in the numbers that represent the results that the system produced. The numbers can tell us that Michael scored much lower than usual, and Dennis scored much higher than usual, but the way to find out what happened, and to improve, is for the team to talk about it. Perhaps Michael was double-teamed. Then a strategy to make the whole team "robust" against that circumstance in the future can be developed.

Consider the difficulty faced by the automobile manufacturer (see Chapter 1) who tried to understand why customers liked or disliked their cars. The engineers thought reductively about the problem: "If I disassemble the whole car into its component parts, I can learn *how* the individual parts perform, then I will know how the whole performs. I can improve the parts, which will improve the whole." Eventually they learned that this approach cannot explain why the whole performs as it does, since it doesn't look at the relationships of the parts to each other and to the purpose of the whole.

The purpose of the orchestra is to "make music." The music is an interaction of many parts–musicians, instruments, theater acoustics, audience sensitivities and expectations, etc. The quality of the performance perceived by the audience, and by the performing artists themselves, depends on how well those parts work together. The quality of the whole depends on the quality of the relationships of the parts. Disassembly of the whole destroys the relationships that give rise to the character of the performance. What characteristics of the parts can be measured that will explain why the whole performs as it does? The quality of relationships, especially human relationships–which is what human enterprise is–cannot be meaningfully quantified. However, they can be discussed in a way that leads to improvement.

IV.

A Framework to Score a Whole In One

Supervision and command are the management of actions; coordination and integration are the management of interactions, and this requires leadership.

Russell Ackoff[33]

THE OWNER-CEO of a successful business told me the following story about one of his manufacturing operations. Each morning the plant manager sat in his orange chair as the six department managers, one by one, came to him with their problems, complaints, and requests. The plant manager acted as the intermediary, a sort of third-party between the department managers. After he retired, each of the six managers wanted his job; they wanted to sit in the orange chair.

The CEO remembered the words of Deming: "An important job of management is to recognize and manage the interdependencies between components. Resolution of conflicts, and removal of barriers to cooperation, are responsibilities of management."[34] He decided that the orange chair process would not continue. If management could not learn to work together, how could they expect others in the organization to do the same. The CEO asked them to work together as a team, but he soon realized that simply asking them was not enough. They continued to point fingers at each other when problems arose, which was often. They had not learned to cooperate, even when the good of the enterprise, and therefore their own good, was at stake. Individual freedom was not sufficient to enable the organization to operate as a whole. Leadership was needed to identify the critical relationships, and then to orchestrate the interactions that characterize those relationships. The framework described below could help him do this.

Two Individuals Make a Relationship

In a system, no matter how large, a relationship is between two people. Let's say that three people–A, B, and C–are in System X (see Figure 7). Three relationships are possible: A and B, A and C, B and C. However, if A and B need to work together, and A and C need to work together, and B and C don't have to work together, then only two of the three possible relationships actually exist.[35] Performance of System X therefore depends on the actions of A, B, and C, and their interactions AB and AC, i.e., X = A + B + C + AB + AC.

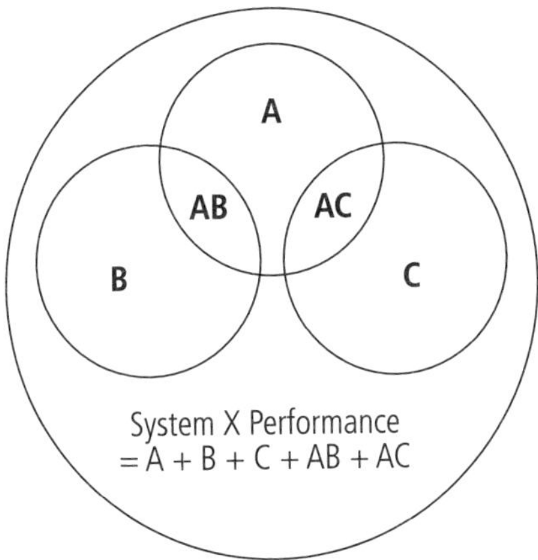

Figure 7. System X: three individuals in two relationships

Orchestrating Interactions in Manufacturing

An engine manufacturing plant of a large automotive business was plagued with a variety of problems, such as product defects and late deliveries to its customer, the assembly plant. The plant manager wanted to improve cooperation in order to eliminate these problems. He knew that continuing to exhort people to do better, or holding more "problem resolution" meetings would not help. Although some of the plant's problems were related to suppliers and to product engineering, he felt that the plant had to clean its own house before he could ask others to improve.

Figure 8 shows engine manufacturing as a system, EM. Four of the contained systems (called departments on traditional organization charts) are located in the engine plant: Production, Human Resources, Plant Engineering, and the Controller. Engine Block Casting is located in the foundry. Performance of the system, EM, depends on:

- Actions within each department in the engine plant: P, H, C, E
- Actions within the production department in the foundry: F
- Interactions of P with the other departments: PH, PC, PE, PF

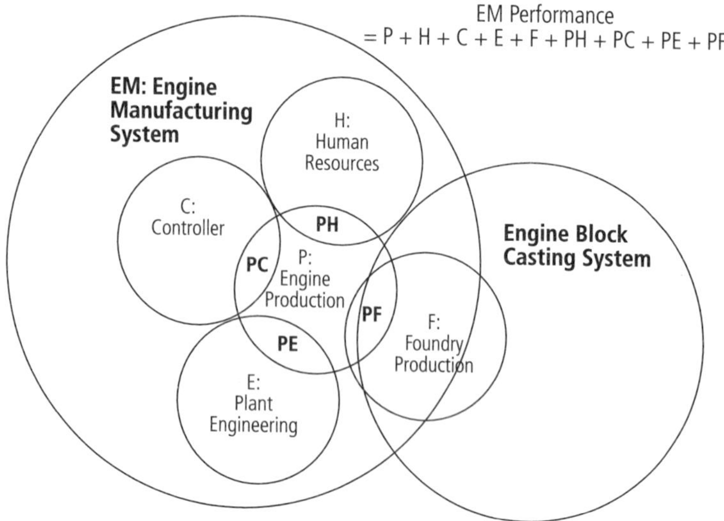

Figure 8. Engine manufacturing viewed as a system

The same kind of map can be applied to look at the sources of performance within any of the contained systems, such as the Controller, or Plant Engineering.

Interactions Matrix

The plant manager asked an internal consultant to help.[36] A two-day planning session was held off-site with department managers and superintendents. The plant manager explained that setting more aggressive objectives would not help the situation because the plant did not have a method to accomplish those objectives. They would have to identify the ways they could support each other. The process started with the manager of Production, who described the difficulties he faced every day to produce high-quality engines and meet the production schedule. He then asked the others how they would help him. Each of the other department managers then proposed, in turn, what they would do to support Production. This was an initial commitment that would continue to be refined as learning occurred. For example:

- The Plant Engineering manager offered to work toward developing a maintenance schedule that would minimize downtime.
- The Controller offered to change the reporting format to move away from micro-reporting of performance on each machine or production area to overall production reporting. The Production manager was given the discretion to develop any kind of measurement and information management system within the department that would help him operate better.

- The Human Resources manager offered to schedule training in Statistical Process Control (SPC).

The initial commitments of these three managers (Foundry Production was not yet involved in this process) to support the Production department are shown in row 1, columns 3–5 of the interactions matrix, Figure 9. Commitments were more detailed than shown here. Only a portion of the matrix is shown.

The process continued as each of the other departments had the chance to explain its situation and receive commitments of support from the others. For example:

- Plant Engineering explained that it was difficult to maintain equipment because there was oil or water on the floor. Also, sometimes they would arrive at the scheduled time and Production would refuse to shut down the machine. The support actions to help Plant Engineering are shown in row 3. Production (row 3,

(1) Department	(2) Production Support Actions	(3) Plant Engineering Support Actions	(4) Controller Support Actions	(5) Human Resources Support Actions
(2) Production (Receiver)	**Within Production**	Meet maintenance schedule.	Accept Production's report format.	Provide SPC training.
(3) Plant Engineering (Receiver)	Shut down machines and clean the area.	**Within Plant Engineering**		
(4) Controller (Receiver)	Provide data in graphical, time-ordered format.		**Within Controller**	

Figure 9. Engine manufacturing system interactions matrix

column 2), for example, agreed to shut down the machines and clean up the area before the scheduled time for maintenance.

- Production (column 2, row 4) offered to provide information to the Controller in time-ordered graphical format. This would enable the Controller to see at a glance whether plant performance is stable and predictable and, therefore, help him to plan.

After the session, each department manager presented the interactions matrix to the supervisors and others within the department. The initial commitments that the manager made on behalf of the department were discussed. In order to develop their capability to meet their commitments, an interactions matrix was developed within each department.

The plant operated for two weeks, with each department working to fulfill its commitments to support the others. Daily meetings with the plant manager moved from frustration and defensiveness to an evaluation of how the system was working. Then the managers met again to look at the commitments they had made. Commitments were modified. This became an ongoing process to learn and improve, and replaced the daily "problem resolution" meetings. Managers no longer were working on problems, they were working on the system to dissolve problems. The role of the plant manager now was one of orchestrating the interactions of the department managers. Likewise, the role of each department manager was to help orchestrate the interactions of people in his or her department, and to facilitate their interactions across departments.

After learning how to operate with this process, the manager of the engine plant asked the foundry manager to use the process. The foundry did so, with success. Eventually the process was used between the foundry and the engine plant. The interactions matrix was expanded to include the production department of the foundry.

V.

A Retail Furniture Business in Concert

The right way to begin to think about the pattern which connects is to think of it as primarily *a dance of interacting parts . . .*

Gregory Bateson[37]

GALLERY FURNITURE OF HOUSTON, TEXAS, is owned and managed by Jim ("Mac") and Linda McIngvale, the couple who started the business in 1981.[38] They grew the company in 10 years into one of the most successful retail furniture businesses in the country, with $40 million in revenue from their only store. Inventory turns were eight times better than the industry average. This feat was accomplished by perfecting the traditional methods of selling furniture and managing the sales force. Mac brought the customers into the store. He became one of the best-recognized personalities in the city mainly because of his frequent appearances in television promotions. Once customers entered the store it was sell, sell, sell. Mac's operating philosophy at that time was "make any sale by any method as long as it's legal."

Mac's management methods assured that this philosophy was followed. Sales associates were individually rewarded or punished according to their performance in meeting Mac's numerical sales targets. Daily contests were held, with bonuses for the best performers. Employees were ranked at the end of the month, with rewards for the top 10 percent and punishment for the bottom 90 percent (the individuals who occupied these positions changed from month to month, so it was actually a lottery, as Mac later realized). This encouraged sales associates to focus on meeting their own needs, not those of the customers. It promoted game playing, such as forcing out deliveries to meet quotas, even if furniture had to be temporarily stored in the sales associate's garage. It encouraged internal competition, such as sales associates failing to wait for their turn (the batting order) to greet a new customer entering the store. Mac thus insured that each sales associate worked as an independent agent. Salespeople were afraid of having to face Mac if they did not make their targets, not only because of the lost compensation and other penalties (e.g., moving to the end of the batting order), but also because Mac could be very intense when he expressed his displeasure. Turnover of sales associates averaged 15 percent a month. Mac had a large budget to continuously advertise for sales associates in the classified section of the Houston newspapers.

Why did customers tolerate the high pressure? Besides the fact that one would face a similar situation in most furniture stores that carried similar merchandise (moderately-priced to moderately high-priced), Mac offered customers an advantage over the competition: The store provided same-day delivery to the Houston metropolitan area.

Constraints on Performance Become Obvious

What changed? Unlike the situation that faces most managers who seek new methods to save them when the business is on the decline, this enterprise was financially successful. However, the store seemed to have reached limits for further growth. Forty-three percent of all customers entering the store purchased goods, compared to an industry average of twenty-five percent. Yet Mac was unable to increase this number, no matter how hard he pushed or cajoled employees. Revenues also had stabilized. Mac wanted to continue to grow. His current location prevented him from adding floor space. In addition, he was the main reason most people shopped there; many customers asked to see him when they came into the store. Mac therefore ruled out opening another location, since he could not be in two places at once.

About this time, Mac became aware of Deming's ideas that numerical quotas and financial incentive schemes discourage cooperation and cause loss. Mac and Linda, together with their managers, attended numerous Deming seminars. Deming helped them to understand how they could go beyond the constraints to their current capability, without adding resources. They were able to envision a business where employees helped each other to sell, where sales personnel were cross-trained in a variety of jobs so they could fill in other parts of the business to meet changing needs (e.g., sell in the store on weekends and holidays when customer volumes were highest, help out in Receiving during vendor deliveries), and where everyone in the company saw themselves as part of a larger whole–the business, and the Houston community. They understood that a deep change in the management system and enterprise culture had to be undertaken. This had to start with Mac himself, but it also required all employees to learn. The first lesson: why it was necessary for sales associates to move from commissions to salary.

Mac's friends warned him that if he did this he would lose the business. Most of the managers and sales associates were afraid of such a change, even though they wanted to be free of the pressure from Mac. They were afraid that they couldn't guarantee success for themselves if they had to depend on others. They had learned well from Mac that *they* were totally responsible for their own performance. Some people worried that others would slack off and not carry their weight. Ironically, each person who worried about someone else also was the target of someone else's worry. Management worried that the *superstars,* the high volume sellers, would leave. Yes, they might, but Mac had come to believe that the overall gain from cooperation would be greater than the losses from exiting superstars. He also understood that the visible gains produced by high pressure superstars are most likely offset by costs, such as when merchandise is returned, or when customer service representatives have to visit the customer to repair damaged merchandise. There is also the loss of repeat customers and all the potential customers that these unhappy customers can persuade to shop elsewhere.

Although Mac had grown the business in the traditional way, he was no longer willing to operate with a system and style that he could now see constrained the potential of the business. He would rather face the problems of change than continue to face the problems produced by the current system.

First a Hop of Faith, Then a Leap

Sales associates and the other employees began attending Deming's seminars. They participated in discussions with Mac and Linda in order to think through the advantages and disadvantages of changing the operating philosophy and management system. In particular, they considered the benefits to the enterprise, and to themselves, of salary pay for sales associates. Mac then took a "hop of faith," as he described it. He eliminated sales quotas. Some salespeople left, as expected. Within a few months, it became obvious that the company was still in business, and that even the small increase in cooperation did raise sales revenues and closing percentages. Fortified by these results, Mac then took a "leap of faith" and replaced commission and bonus pay of the sales force with salary pay. Current employees were given a salary based on the prior year earnings and seniority. New employees were given a starting salary, which had been established by Mac and a study team from the sales department. Even though the new compensation system included profit sharing and medical benefits, some more sales people left. Those who stayed still may have had some reservations so early into the change, but they found that they liked the predictable income versus the weekly and monthly ups and downs they experienced under commission pay.

One consequence of this change was a self-selection process. Individuals who stayed, as well as new hires, were able to work more cooperatively. These individuals also were able to easily move away from hard-sell tactics and take on a more professional approach of helping to identify and meet customers' needs. The character of the system was indeed beginning to change.

People See the Business as a Whole System

Mac (CEO, and General Manager of the store) and Linda (General Manager of the Distribution Center) met with employees to discuss the business as a system (see Figure 10). This discussion helped management see that critical interdependencies had to be identified so that proper working relationships could be established. Consistent with the ending of sales quotas for individuals, management's role would move away from the management of the actions of individuals to achieve sales objectives, toward an orchestration of interactions that would benefit the business as a whole. Everyone agreed that every aspect of the customer's experience must be very positive. Customers must feel "wow" in every interaction they have with any part of the business.

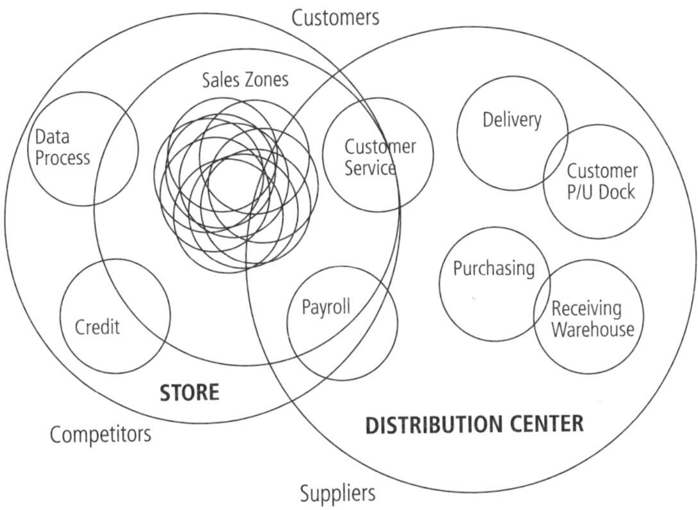

Figure 10. Furniture business viewed as a system

Interactions Matrix

Management of the store met with the consultant to discuss the process of interactions management that would be used to develop a system of mutual support and cooperation. Each manager then met with his or her area (e.g., Sales Zones, Credit, Data Processing) to prepare a description of what they faced every day, which they later would share with the other areas. Mac and the managers then met together to develop the interactions matrix for the store. Participants alternated between two roles, receiver partner and provider partner, following the guidelines shown below.

Receiver Partner Guidelines

Your role as receiver partner is to help others gain an appreciation for your situation, including the daily problems, obstacles, challenges, and requirements you face. Therefore:

1. *Do* tell the others enough about your situation so that they will be able to determine how they can help you. *Do not* tell the others, "I want you to do this for me. If you do this for me and that for me everything will be OK."
2. *Do* provide some examples to give others an appreciation for the general situation you face and the consequences to the organization. *Do not* develop a long list of problems. The point here is not to list every problem that you face. Your specific problems are symptoms of a broader system problem, which this process is trying to define and dissolve.
3. *Do* prioritize your concerns in order of importance. *Do not* try to overwhelm the others with the incredible difficulties you face, as if your situation were worse than theirs.
4. *Do* raise issues that you really think are out of your control to influence, where you really need the help of others. *Do not* raise issues that are within your control to influence. (You may not see this at first.)

5. *Do not* point fingers, assign blame, or shift the burden to others. You are part of the system and so are the others. Remember, most of what happens is produced by the system. Bad things happen even when people want to do a good job and try their best. *We are trying to get at the system problems.*

Provider Partner Guidelines

Your role as provider partner is to offer support actions to help others, in the context of the larger system. Therefore:

1. *Avoid* thinking "Yes, I would like to help, but . . . ." Initially, do not put limits on how you can help others. You may think you do not have the ability to help others, but after initial development of the matrix you may find you can do more because the others will support you in new ways. You certainly do not want to over commit, but you should try not to under commit.
2. *Avoid* the self-fulfilling prophecy where each individual is afraid to trust the other. Do trust others.

After reviewing the guidelines, each manager had a chance to explain the situation in his or her area, using the information each had prepared earlier. For example:

- The Credit Department manager explained that information often was missing from the credit application that Sales submitted to them. When this happened, Credit had to chase down the sales associate before they could complete the credit check.

- A common problem was revealed after the Sales Zone managers described their situation: Customers were turned over from one sales zone to another without introducing the customer to the sales associate in that area. Customers were annoyed at having to answer the same kinds of questions each time they moved to another area of the store.

After a manager described the situation for his or her area, the others offered ways in which they would help, following the guidelines for the role of provider partner. A portion of the interactions matrix for the store is shown in Figure 11. The Bedding Sales Zone (row 2, column 1) is supported by the actions of the other Sales Zones (row 2, column 2), and by Data Processing (row 2, column 3). Part of the situation that Data Processing faces each day is shown in the shaded cell (row 3, column 3). Sales offered to help Credit (row 3, column 2).

(1) Area or Department	(2) Sales Zones Support Actions (Provider Partner)	(3) Data Processing Support Actions (Provider Partner)
(2) Bedding Sales Zone (Receiver Partner)	Ask customers if they have been to Bedding. If not, ask if they would like to be escorted there.	Remind customers, if they purchased lamps, to take them with them. Ask customers who purchased bedroom furniture if they need a new bed frame or mattress.
(3) Data Processing (Receiver Partner)	Put correct SKU numbers on work sheets and complete all items. Give priority to pages from Credit.	Within Data Processing work sheets illegible and incomplete. Sales associates slow to respond to paging.

Figure 11. Interactions matrix for store

The process used within the store was repeated with the management of the distribution center. A portion of the interactions matrix is shown in Figure 12.

After learning how to operate according to these mutual commitments, the matrix was expanded to include interactions between the store and the distribution center.

A Leap of Performance

The transformation of the system, which included the orchestration of relationships described here, produced dramatic improvements in performance in about three years. For example, sales revenues increased from $40 million to $70 million, closing percentages and inventory turns were up, the cost of sales decreased, and turnover was nearly eliminated. The flexibility to move employees on and off the sales floor to meet changing situations, made it unnecessary to hire just-in-case sales people. Conversely, since many sales associates were trained in other functions, e.g., delivery and customer service, they were able to help out during the week during slower sales

(1) Area or Department	(2) Customer Delivery Support Actions (Provider Partner)	(3) Purchasing Support Actions (Provider Partner)
(2) Customer Service (Receiver Partner)		Order only merchandise that manufacturer will service, not one-time-only merchandise.
(3) Receiving Warehouse (Receiver Partner)	Identify exchanged or returned merchandise on paperwork as "return to vendor" or "restock."	

Figure 12. Interactions matrix for distribution center

periods. Other costs inherent in the old management system began to disappear, e.g., merchandise returns and other costs due to overselling the customers. More time was spent on work that added value, e.g., the time Payroll needed to administer the pay system was reduced from ten hours for commission to one hour for salary pay. In addition, Payroll no longer had to deal with a continual stream of phone calls (about 300 per week) from sales associates asking if they made quota. Profits increased and were shared with employees. Customers felt less pressured and helped more.

Ongoing Learning of Individuals and Evolution of the Enterprise

This was a momentous change, not just for the business, but personally for Mac. He was fully aware that he occasionally reverted back to his old, hard-driving style, but this happened less often as time went by. Yet it was still a source of fear in the organization. A key role of the external consultant was to make Mac aware of this tendency to revert, understand its source, see its potential to destroy the new system he put in place, and work on minimizing it.

People began to identify themselves not so much by their function, but as a part of Gallery Furniture. The thought, "that's not my job," was disappearing. Decisions were made jointly by the people affected. Seasoned sales associates helped new ones. Instead of spending time pouring over computer printouts of sales and commissions, people had time and energy to work on improvement and standardization of processes, and to improve their personal sales techniques. Mac also began to introduce these practices to his suppliers through in-house seminars.

VI.

A Custom Job Shop in Concert

A good manager is like a symphony conductor . . . trying to bring out of that group a wide range of simultaneous and harmonic tones and sounds. It is a dynamic process.

General (Ret.) Robert T. Herres[39]

THE COMPANY designs and manufactures vinyl extrusions to meet the needs of window and door system manufacturers who supply the commercial and home building industries. It is privately owned by the CEO, who started the business around 1970. The company has the capability under one roof to custom design product, custom design and manufacture the tools and dies, and then manufacture the final product.

The CEO, President, and all of the managers attended a four-day seminar of W. Edwards Deming. They came to believe that the management principles and methods that he presented would help the company to improve. The company advertised this to the world in its public statements and marketing literature, which read in part: "We follow the principles of the late Dr. W. Edwards Deming . . . . Dr. Deming's teachings guide us to focus on continual improvement of product quality and customer service . . . . The most important relationships are supplier-customer interactions, as well as the relationships between the people of (company name)."

The efforts described below to break down barriers between departments (Deming's Point Number 9) were part of a larger process of change that included many other activities, such as redesign of the compensation system.

Management had decided that in order to continue to grow and to differentiate itself from its competitors it had to produce at least one new die each day to accommodate the schedules of its current customers and meet commitments to new customers. This "fact of life," this reality of the business, had been translated into a numerical objective for the manager of Tooling Design and Manufacture. The capability to consistently achieve this objective had not yet been demonstrated.

The manager of Tooling Design and Manufacture met once or twice a week with his boss, the company President, to evaluate how he was doing with regard to the objective. Progress was not being made. The department manager was quite frustrated, first, because he knew the importance of meeting the objective, and second, because every day he encountered obstacles to meeting the objective. He knew that performance would improve if there was more cooperation between departments, for example, if he could get more frequent access to production equipment to test the dies before releasing them to Production.

Since the Production manager was under pressure to meet his own numerical objectives, he was not very willing to give up machine time.

Every day there were many interactions between members of management, mainly in the form of meetings, mostly ad hoc, except for the weekly management meeting with the President. These interactions were not as cooperative as they needed to be to improve the performance of the business. Occasionally an attitude of provincialism surfaced as one department revealed its belief that it was more important than the others, or had a more difficult job than the others, or that the others were not doing their job.

Production Tooling: The System in Focus

The external consultant[40] and one of the managers drew a picture (see Figure 13) to illustrate how the various departments influenced the capability of the company to produce dies. The system in focus is the Production Tooling System. The Advanced Tooling Development System is also shown to illustrate that people usually participate in more than one system.

The system generally operates in the following manner. Sales interests a new customer, usually a window manufacturer, in the capabilities of the company. Then Product Design works with the customer to develop a design that meets that customer's requirements. Computer aided design (CAD) technology is used. The product

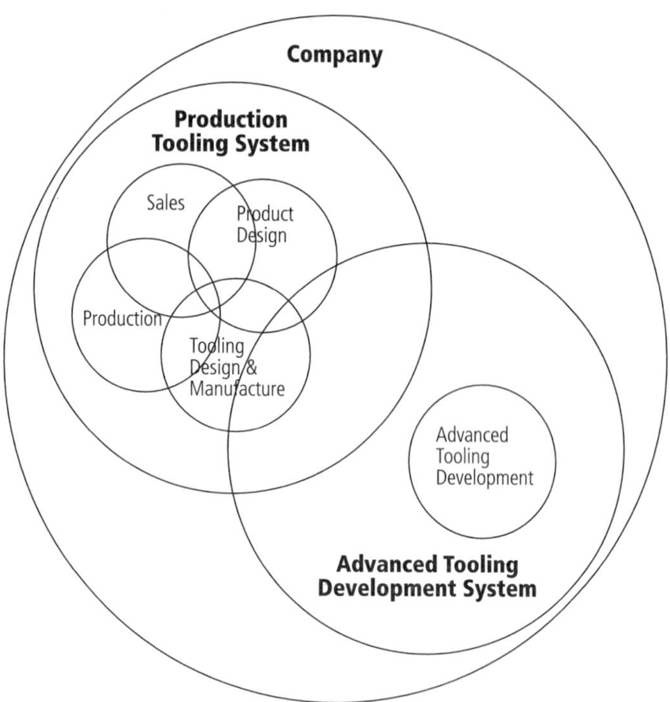

Figure 13. Production tooling system

design is then submitted to the Tool Design and Manufacture department, where it is translated through CAD to a blueprint which will be used to manufacture the die. The die is then manufactured by highly-skilled people who use computer-controlled, high-precision metal-working equipment. The die is tested on production equipment. Then the die is sent to Production, where it is used for the initial and subsequent customer orders. The die is placed in an extruder. Plastic compound material is fed in, heated to the proper temperature, extruded as a continuous molded strip, and cut to a standard length. These are bundled and shipped to the customer, who will cut them into the lengths required to fabricate windows.

After considering the system view of the company, the President agreed to support a process to improve the capability of the system to manufacture production-ready dies. This would require him to change his role from one of establishing objectives for individuals and managing their actions to meet those objectives, to one of orchestrating the interactions of the managers in the system.

Interactions Matrix

Each manager played the dual roles of provider partner and receiver partner, using the method described in Chapter 5. Each manager began to get a greater appreciation for what the others faced. After each session, the matrix was updated and distributed. Managers were asked to review their commitments of support to each other to make sure that they were consistent with the aim to increase the number of new dies produced. The group finally agreed to operate by the interactions matrix, partially shown in Figure 14. In columns 2–5 of each row are the actions of each manager to support the manager shown in column 1 of the row. The shaded cells contain the description from the manager of the situation within the department.

Improvements were reflected in results and in relationships between departments. Daily interactions, and the

(1) Department	(2) Sales Support Actions (Provider Partner)	(3) Product Design Support Actions (Provider Partner)	(4) Tooling Design & Manufacture Support Actions (Provider Partner)	(5) Production Support Actions (Provider Partner)
(2) Sales (Receiver Partner)	Not well informed about production schedule changes in order to manage relationships with customer.	Simplify designs to speed up tool production and meet customer schedule.	Provide current tool schedules to Sales and update on progress.	Plan for flexibility to meet short lead-time requests.
(3) Product Design (Receiver Partner)	Work with customer to minimize customer changes to design.	No relief to deal with post-approval design changes by customer, Tooling, or Production.	Provide feedback on tooling feasibility for product design.	Provide production samples of prior designs to show produceability of a proposed design.
(4) Tooling Design & Manufacture (Receiver Partner)	Communicate possible changes to schedule by customer.	Work with Tooling and customer to simplify product design for tooling.	Production extruders not available to test tools.	Coordinate with Tooling to make extruders available to test tools.
(5) Production (Receiver Partner)	Work with customers to develop realistic timing.	Work with Tooling and customer to simplify product design for tooling.	Use SPC on tool cutting equipment to build better tools.	Dies need frequent maintenance.

Figure 14. Production tooling system interactions matrix

weekly management meeting with the President reflected a new sense of "being in it together." The meeting was a chance for them to evaluate how well they and others in the company were working together as a system, and to update the matrix. Management agreed to extend this method to other systems.

VII.

A Corporate Staff in Concert[41]

Somehow, a curious union of opposites has to occur where performers have to find creative freedom in the closely interconnected workings of the system.

Peter B. Vaill[42]

Leaders learn to make a commitment to the common good. . . . When you think ethically about this, individual freedom becomes difficult to justify unless it results ultimately in the common good.

Max DePree[43]

THE ENTERPRISE is composed of subsidiary companies that provide a variety of telecommunications and information products and services, primarily local and long distance phone service, mobile-cellular products and services, directory information, and advertising. A central staff provides corporate policies and guidance and carries out other corporate functions.

Senior management wanted the company to become adaptable and flexible in dealing with an external environment of dramatic change (e.g., regulations, technology, competitors). Internally it sought to develop collaboration, teamwork, listening, and trust. The two executive vice presidents who presided over the corporate staff wanted to see these values operationalized throughout the company so that the firm could take greater advantage of the information, knowledge, and talent that existed in the separate parts of the enterprise. They wanted the enterprise to operate as one interrelated business (see Figure 15), rather than as independent parts in the manner of a holding company.

The two staff executives recognized that one could not simply preach to others about change; change had to start with oneself, whether as an individual or as an organization. Therefore, the staff first would have to learn

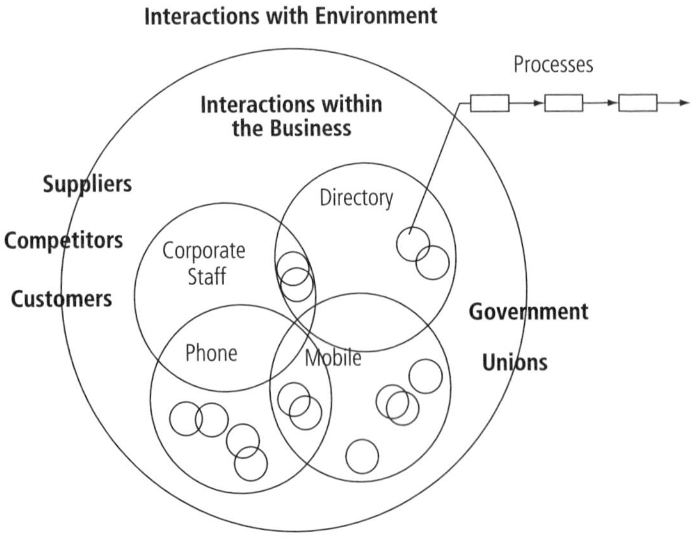

Figure 15. A whole-system view of the business

how to operate according to the values and principles that they wanted others in the company to follow. Interactions between staff functions tended to occur only by way of requests to other staff departments for information, or responses to such requests from those departments. Management agreed to proceed with development of a process to identify and manage key relationships within the staff.

Interactions Matrix

Participants were the two staff executive vice presidents and their department heads. They followed a process similar to that described in previous chapters. Each individual participant played the roles of provider partner and receiver partner. The commitment of the senior staff executives made it possible to bring together, in the same room at the same time, the management of the whole system. The managers, however, did not quite see themselves as parts of a system at the start of the process.

An initial session was held to develop mutual understanding and commitments of support in the form of an interactions matrix. After the session, the preliminary matrix was distributed to the participants. They were asked to complete the matrix regarding their own needs for support from others, and their commitments to support others. The matrix then was modified to include this new information. A second meeting was held with all of the managers to review the updated matrix.

(1) Department	(2) Treasury Support Actions (Provider Partner)	(3) Human Resources Support Actions (Provider Partner)	(5) Investor Relations Support Actions (Provider Partner)
(2) Treasury (Receiver Partner)	Timely information on long-term and short-term plans of each business area. Knowledge of risks inherent in plans.	Involve Treasury early in design of new compensation and benefits programs.	Assist in evaluation of external information sources.
(3) Human Resources (Receiver Partner)	Provide information and analysis to support development of compensation plan.	HR policies and processes must support business strategy and corporate values.	Provide employee seminars on stock investing.
(4) Investor Relations (Receiver Partner)	Provide information on financing plans and activities. Cooperate in shareholder related activity.	Identify significant HR initiatives to enable effective external positioning within the invest-ment community. Respond effectively to HR related questions.	Maintain credibility with external analysts and investors. Respond quickly to ad hoc questions from other departments.

Figure 16. Interactions matrix for corporate staff

Figure 16 presents a portion of the matrix for three areas. The shaded cells show the requirements within a department. A non-shaded entry shows the commitment of support by the manager indicated at the top of columns 2–4 to another manager, indicated in rows 2–4, column 1.

Hidden Critical Interdependencies Are Revealed

The completed interactions matrix was examined by the Human Resources Director, whose purview encompassed the entire staff. He concluded that more interdependencies should logically exist but had not been revealed. He thought that each manager might find it easier to identify additional interdependencies if he or she considered four generic staff activities:

- (P): Planning organization-wide. Develop plans that affect all of the business or all of the corporate staff.
- (R): Regulating. Develop and monitor rules and regulations, e.g., company policy.
- (S): Stakeholder positioning. Influence external stakeholders, e.g., government, investors, the public.
- (D): Service delivery. Provide a service to another staff department or subsidiary business.

(1) Department	(2) Business Planning Function-Process	(3) Accounting Function-Process	(5) Public Relations Function-Process
(2) Business Development	P, R, D	-----	D
(3) Controller	R, D	P, R, S, D	-----
(4) Public Affairs	S	-----	P, R, S, D

Figure 17. Function-process activity matrix

The Human Resources Director developed a Function-Process Activity Matrix, partially shown in Figure 17. Three departments are shown in column 1, rows 2–4. Three functions, or processes, are shown in columns 2–4. The entries within each cell indicate which generic staff activities each department in column 1 has to perform to do its work. The shaded cell in each row indicates that the department has the primary responsibility to carry out the function listed at the top of the column. It therefore engages in most of the generic staff activities in order to manage that function or process. Business Development, (row 2, shaded cell), for example, performs activities P, R, D. The non-shaded cells indicate an overlap of staff activities. Public Affairs (row 4) performs a business planning function (column 2) through its activities, indicated by "S," to influence external stakeholders. Therefore, Public Affairs and Business Development should be able to help each other.

Managers Participating	Partnership X	Partnership Y	Partnership Z	Number of Partnerships that Contain the Manager
A	•	•		2
B	•		•	2
C		•		1
D			•	1
E		•		1
Number of Managers in the Partnership	2	3	2	7

Figure 18. Formation of staff partnerships

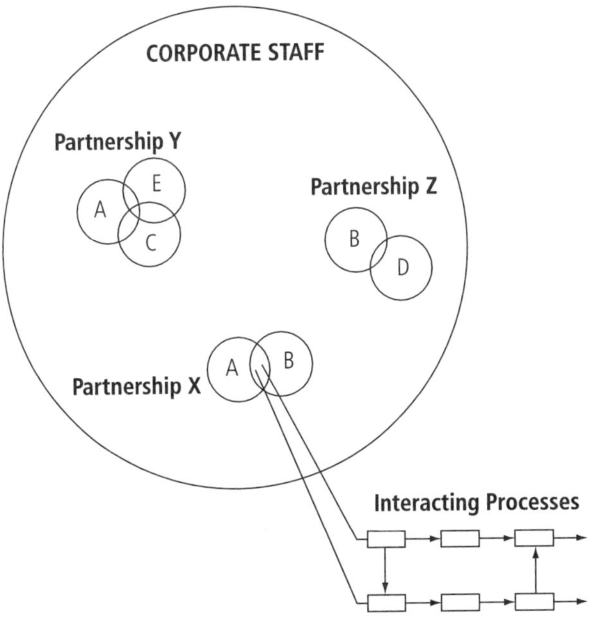

Figure 19. Staff partnerships

Partnerships Are Formed

The Function-Process Activity Matrix helped to reveal the basis for additional relationships. A partnership concept was developed to enable those managers in the most critical interdependencies to work together (see Figure 18). The managers decided to limit their participation to a maximum of three partnerships at any one time. Figure 19 illustrates the partnerships identified in Figure 18.

Learning Continues

Some partnerships are insensitive to short-term environmental changes and will exist for a relatively long time. Others will be formed to adapt to specific changes in the environment, since the company will be affected by communications technology and by government policies and regulations. Regular meetings of all staff management were held to share information about partnership activities and developments in the environmental suprasystem that could change interdependencies and therefore require new partnership arrangements. They also discussed how various interaction management issues were handled within a partnership, e.g., how often to meet, how to manage the process as it starts to involve more employees within each department.

References

1. Russell L. Ackoff, *The Democratic Corporation,* New York, New York: Oxford University Press, 1994, pp. 32–33.
2. Gregory Bateson and Mary Catherine Bateson, *Angels Fear: Towards an Epistemology of the Sacred,* New York, New York: Bantam Books, 1988, p. 161.
3. Alfred Korzybski, *Science and Sanity*, Lakeville, Connecticut: The International Non-Aristotelian Library Publishing Company, 1933.
4. W. Edwards Deming, *Out of the Crisis*, Cambridge Massachusetts: MIT-CAES, 1986, Chapter 9, pp. 276–296.
5. See, for example, the following books: Chris Argyris, *Overcoming Organizational Defenses: Facilitating Organizational Learning*, Boston: Allyn and Bacon, 1990; Peter M. Senge, *The Fifth Discipline: The Art and Practice of the Learning Organization*, New York, New York: Doubleday/Currency, 1990; Peter M. Senge, et al., *The Fifth Discipline Fieldbook*, New York, New York: Doubleday/Currency, 1994.
6. See for example, R. Buckminster Fuller, *Synergetics: Explorations in the Geometry of Thinking*, New York, New York: Macmillan Publishing Company, 1975.

7. Based on table in W. Edwards Deming, *The New Economics,* Second Edition, Cambridge, Massachusetts: MIT–CAES, 1994, p. 67.

8. See the following discussions of performance and compensation: W. Edwards Deming, *Out of the Crisis,* Cambridge Massachusetts: MIT–CAES, 1986, pp. 101–126; Brian L. Joiner, *Fourth Generation Management,* New York, New York: McGraw-Hill, 1994, pp. 235–249; Joyce Orsini, "Bonuses: What is the Impact?," *National Productivity Review,* Spring, 1987, 180–184; Peter R. Scholtes, *The Leader's Handbook,* New York: McGraw-Hill, 1998, pp. 293–368.

9. W. Edwards Deming, *The New Economics,* Second Edition, Cambridge, Massachusetts: MIT-CAES, 1994, p. 50.

10. H. Thomas Johnson, "A Different Perspective on Quality: Bringing Management to Life," keynote presentation to the W. Edwards Deming Institute Fall Conference, October, 1997.

11. Margaret J. Wheatley, "De-engineering The Corporation," *Industry Week,* April 18, 1994, p. 18.

12. Russell L. Ackoff, *The Democratic Corporation,* New York, New York: Oxford University Press, 1994, pp. 32–33.

13. Gregory Bateson, *Mind and Nature: A Neccessary Unity,* New York, New York: Bantam Books, 1988.

14. Margaret J. Wheatley, *Leadership and the New Science,* San Francisco, California: Berrett-Koehler, 1992.

15. Michael Rothschild, *Bionomics: Economy as Ecosystem*, New York, New York: Henry Holt and Company, 1990, pp. 39–40.

16. Gregory Bateson, *Steps to an Ecology of Mind*, New York, New York: Ballantine Books, 1972, pp. 450–451.

17. Fritjof Capra, *The Web of Life*, New York, New York: Anchor Books Doubleday, 1996, p. 6–7.

18. Adam Smith, *An Inquiry Into The Nature and Causes of The Wealth of Nations*, New York, New York: The Modern Library, 1937, p. 423.

19. Fritjof Capra, *The Web of Life*, New York, New York: Anchor Books Doubleday, 1996, p. 62.

20. Michael Rothschild, *Bionomics: Economy as Ecosystem*, New York, New York: Henry Holt and Company, 1990, p. 336.

21. Alfie Kohn, *No Contest: The Case Against Competition*, Boston: Houghton Mifflin Company, 1986.

22. Stephen Jay Gould, "The Wheel of Fortune and the Wedge of Progress," *Natural History*, March, 1989, 14–21. This short paper provides an example of Gould's thinking.

23. See for example, Sharon Danann, "Cracking the Electronic Whip," *Harpers Magazine*, August, 1990, pp. 18–19.

24. For a thorough discussion of the subject see Alfie Kohn, *Punished by Rewards*, New York, New York: Houghton Mifflin Company, 1993.

25. Michael Polanyi and Harry Prosch, *Meaning,* Chicago, Illinois: The University of Chicago Press, 1975, pp. 182–216.

26. W. Edwards Deming, *The New Economics,* Second Edition, Cambridge, Massachusetts: MIT-CAES, 1994, pp. 96–97.

27. Max DePree, *Leadership Jazz,* New York, New York: DoubleDay Currency, 1992, pp. 156–157.

28. Ibid, p. 44.

29. Ibid, p. 103.

30. Robertson Davies, *Fifth Business,* New York, New York: The Viking Press, 1970, p. 261.

31. Robert K. Greenleaf, *Servant Leadership: The Nature of Legitimate Power and Greatness,* New York, New York: Paulist Press, 1977.

32. Peter B. Vaill, *Managing as a Performing Art: New Ideas for a World of Chaotic Change,* San Francisco, California: Josey-Bass, 1989, p. 124.

33. Russell L. Ackoff, *The Democratic Corporation,* New York, New York: Oxford University Press, 1994, p. 22.

34. W. Edwards Deming, *The New Economics,* Second Edition, Cambridge, Massachusetts: MIT-CAES, 1994, p. 64.

35. The number of relationships possible is calculated using the formula for combinations, $n = \frac{1}{2}[n \times (n - 1)]$, where n is the number of individuals in the system. For example: if there are two people in the system, only one relationship is possible (obviously) since $n = \frac{1}{2}[2 \times (2 - 1)] = 1$; if there are four people, then six relationships are possible, since $n = \frac{1}{2}[4 \times (4 - 1)] = 6$; and so on. A relationship may be possible, but not necessary for the system. Within a relationship, many interactions are possible.

36. Dr. Jaime A. Hermann designed and facilitated the process.

37. Gregory Bateson, *Mind and Nature: A Necessary Unity*, New York, New York: Bantam Books, 1988, p. 13.

38. This enterprise is identified by name because Mac has given many public talks about changes in the business. The author consulted to the company.

39. General Robert T. Herres, Chairman and CEO of USAA, *Aide Magazine,* December, 1993, p. 8.

40. The author.

41. The author was the consultant.

42. Peter B. Vaill, *Managing as a Performing Art: New Ideas for a World of Chaotic Change,* San Francisco, California: Josey-Bass, 1989, p. 124.

43. Max DePree, *Leadership Jazz,* New York, New York: Doubleday Currency, 1992, p. 138.

Further Reading

Bateson, Gregory. *Mind and Nature: A Necessary Unity*. New York, New York: Bantam Books, 1988.

Deming, W. Edwards. *Out of the Crisis*. Cambridge, Massachusetts: MIT-CAES, 1986.

Deming, W. Edwards. *The New Economics*, Second Edition, Cambridge, Massachusetts: MIT-CAES, 1994.

DePree, Max. *Leadership Jazz*. New York, New York: Currency Doubleday, 1992.

Vaill, Peter B. *Managing as a Performing Art: New Ideas for a World of Chaotic Change*. San Francisco, California, Josey-Bass, 1989.

Wheatley, Margaret J. *Leadership and the New Science*. San Francisco, California, Berrett-Koeher, 1992.

About the Author

Ed Baker was with the Ford Motor Company from 1972–1992. He was Director, Quality Strategy and Operations Support, for Ford from 1987–1992 where he "orchestrated" the interaction of Dr. W. Edwards Deming with the Company.

He was responsible for the development and application of methods to improve quality and strengthen competitive position of Ford's businesses worldwide. Ed worked with Dr. Deming from 1981–1993 and assisted him in more than 70 public and private seminars.

Dr. Baker consults to a variety of enterprises. He received his M.B.A. from the Baruch School of Business Administration of the City University of New York and his Ph.D. in Industrial and Organization Psychology from Bowling Green State University, Ohio. He was an Aspen Institute Senior Fellow from 1992–1995. His other writings include, "Managing Human Performance," a section in *Juran's Quality Control Handbook* (Fourth Edition), and "Springing Ourselves from the Measurement Trap," in Peter Senge et al., *The Fifth Discipline Fieldbook.*

Ed Baker
P.O. Box 5797
Scottsdale, Arizona 85261
USA